	DATE DUE		
MAY 17 '93			
OCT 14 '95			
NOV 4 - '95			
SEP 9 '96			
JUL 1 9 1997			
APR 0 7 1999			
MAR 1 3 2000			
APR. 3 0 2003			
OCT 0 2 2009			
MAR 0 3 2011			

Junior Science

weather

Terry Jennings

Illustrations by David Anstey

Gloucester Press
New York · London · Toronto · Sydney

About this book

You can learn many things about the weather in this book – what clouds and fog are, why rain and snow fall and how winds are formed. There are lots of experiments and activities for you to try. You will find out how to make a rain gauge, a temperature chart, a windsock and much more.

First published in the United States in 1988 by Gloucester Press 387 Park Avenue South New York, NY 10016

ISBN 0 531 10788 8

Library of Congress Catalog Card Number: 87-82974

© BLA Publishing Limited 1988

This book was designed and produced by BLA Publishing Limited, TR House, Christopher Road, East Grinstead, Sussex, England. A member of the Ling Kee Group London Hong Kong Taipei Singapore New York

Printed in Spain by Heraclio Fournier, S.A.

14456

Look outside your window and see what it is like today. It may be wet or dry or windy or still. It may be hot or cold or sunny or cloudy. These are some of the changes we call weather. The picture shows a cold and windy scene. The leaves are blowing off the trees so it must be fall.

We wear thick, warm clothes in cold weather. We wear lighter, thinner clothes in hot weather. Look at these two pictures. Think about what kind of clothing you would wear if you were in the pictures.

Draw two pictures of yourself on a piece of paper. Show the clothes you wear when it is cold and the clothes you wear when it is hot and sunny.

4

This is a thermometer. It is used to measure the temperature. The thermometer shows how hot or cold the air is. The thermometer in the picture shows a temperature of 20°C (68°F).

You could make a temperature chart like this. Each morning for a week take a thermometer outside. Wait a few minutes and read the temperature.

Mark the temperature on the chart. At the end of the week you will see which day was the warmest and which day was the coldest.

You could also make a Weather Notebook. Each day write down the date on a clean page. Write down what the weather is like. You could even draw a little picture to show what the weather is like. Then write down the temperature.

Wednesday July 31
It is sunny and the sky is blue.
The temperature is 68°F

Take different kinds of containers and put them out in the rain. You will see that different amounts of rain will fall in the containers. In the picture, the container which caught the most rain was the plastic box. The water was deepest in the tumbler. The baking pan would be the first to overflow.

You can make a rain gauge to show how much rain falls. Ask a grown-up to cut the top off a plastic bottle. Put the top back on the bottle upside down. Stand the rain gauge outside and put bricks around it to stop the wind blowing it over.

Each morning look at the rain gauge to see how much rain has fallen. Put each day's rain into a little bottle. Use a different bottle every day. The bottles in the picture hold one week's rain. You can see that most rain fell on Tuesday and no rain fell on Sunday and Thursday.

Go out after it has rained and look for a puddle.
Draw a chalk line around the puddle. If the next
day is sunny you will see that the puddle is
smaller. Some of the water has dried up in the
sun. The water has turned into a gas called
water vapor which goes into the air.

The warmth of a room will also turn water into water vapor. You can see this if you stand a saucer of water on a windowsill. The next day look at the saucer. Some of the water will have disappeared.

All over the world water is drying up and going into the air as water vapor. We cannot see water vapor. But high in the sky where it is cold, water vapor turns to little drops of water. These tiny drops of water form clouds. Clouds are rather like steam.

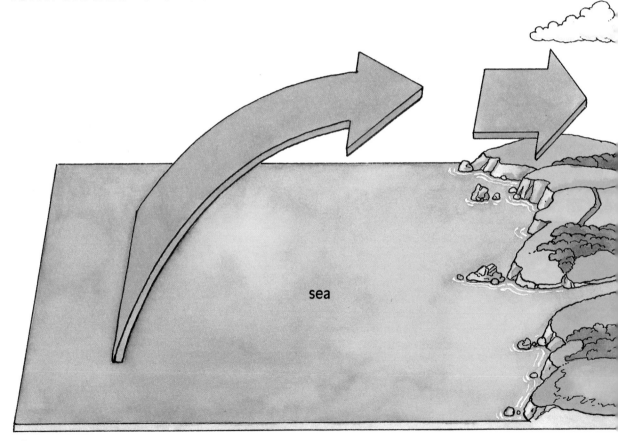

sea

Sometimes clouds come right down to the ground. Then there is mist or fog. Sometimes the tiny drops of water join together. Then they fall as rain. If it is very cold high in the sky, the drops of water may freeze and form ice. Then they fall as snow.

clouds

rain

Look at the sky on a sunny day.
There may be small white
clouds in the sky. Look at the
sky on a rainy day. The clouds
will be dark and gray and they
may cover the sky.
Draw a picture of a cloudy day.
Write down what kind of weather
it is when you see the clouds.

Make a cloud frame like this out of black paper. Stick it to a window and look at the clouds. You will be able to see how quickly they pass by. It is the wind that makes the clouds move along.

15

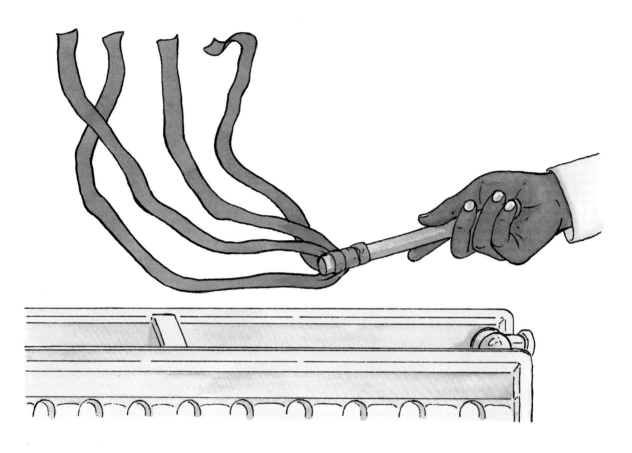

Cut some tissue paper into thin strips and stick
them onto a stick. Hold the strips over a hot
radiator and they will move. They move because
a radiator heats the air above it. This hot air is
lighter. Cooler air rushes in and pushes the warm
air upward. The warm air moves the strips as it rises.

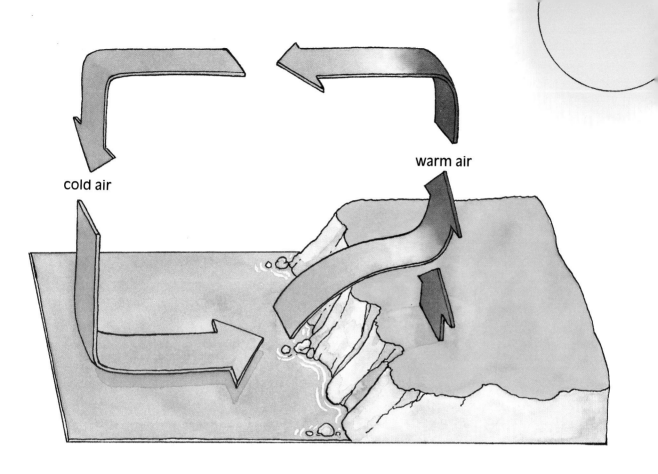

cold air

warm air

The same sort of thing happens all over the world. The sun warms the land. The land warms the air above it. The warm air is lighter. Cold air moves in and pushes the warm air upward. That is how winds are formed. Winds are moving air.

This is a picture of a busy airport. The windsock on the right shows which way the wind is blowing.

You can make a windsock from a pair of pantyhose. Ask a grown-up to help. Cut a piece from one of the legs and thread a loop of wire through it. Tie three pieces of string to the wire. Then push a long stick into the grass. Knock a nail into the top of the stick and tie the windsock to the nail. The wind will fill the windsock. A compass will show in which direction the wind is blowing.

You can also measure how hard the wind is blowing. Stick four paper cups to a paper plate. Paint one of the cups red. Fasten the paper plate to the top of a stick by a nail at the center. Blow on one of the cups. The plate will turn. The harder the wind blows, the faster the wind measurer will turn. You can tell how fast the wind is blowing by counting how many turns the red cup makes in one minute.

Look at the picture. It is snowing. The snow falls in little pieces called snowflakes. Snowflakes are made of ice.

Try catching some snowflakes on a piece of black paper. Look at them with a hand lens to see what they look like.

Cut some snowflakes like these from silver paper. You could hang them in your classroom or bedroom.

21

Go outside early one morning. You might find
that the grass is covered with little drops of
water. This is called dew. It is formed when
the air cools at night. Then some of the water
vapor in the air turns into water and collects
on plants, stones and cars.

Sometimes on very cold nights water vapor
in the air freezes and turns to little pieces of
ice. Everything is then covered by a white
frost. On very cold nights, water on the roads
freezes and turns to dangerous ice.

glossary

Here are the meanings of some words you may have used for the first time in this book.

cloud: a mass of tiny water drops floating in the air.

dew: tiny drops of water formed on cool surfaces out of doors during the night.

fog: a cloud at ground level.

frost: white, powdery ice which forms at night in very cold weather.

mist: a cloud of very fine water drops floating in the air near the ground or over the sea.

rain gauge: an instrument that measures rainfall.

snow: soft white pieces of ice that fall to the ground as snowflakes.

temperature: the hotness or coldness of something.

thermometer: an instrument for measuring temperature.

water vapor: a gas formed by warming water.

wind: a movement of air.

index

clothes 4

cloud 12, 13, 14, 15, 23

cloud frame 15

dew 22, 23

fall 3

fog 13, 23

frost 22, 23

ice 13, 21, 22

mist 13, 23

puddle 10

rain 7, 8, 9, 10, 13

rain gauge 8, 9, 23

snow 13, 21, 23

sun 10, 17

temperature 5, 6, 23

thermometer 5, 23

water vapor 10, 11, 12, 22, 23

weather notebook 6

wind 8, 15, 17, 18, 20, 23

wind measurer 20

windsock 18